DIPLODOCUS

by Nick Hunter

T0387469

Consultant: Mathew J. Wedel, PhD
Western University of Health Sciences
Pomona, California

PEBBLE
a capstone imprint

Published by Pebble, an imprint of Capstone
1710 Roe Crest Drive, North Mankato, Minnesota 56003
capstonepub.com

Library of Congress Cataloging-in-Publication Data is available on the Library of Congress website.

ISBN: 9798875226786 (hardcover)
ISBN: 9798875234125 (paperback)
ISBN: 9798875234132 (ebook PDF)

Summary: Describes Diplodocus, where it lived, what it ate, how it behaved, how it was discovered, and more.

Editorial Credits
Designer: Dina Her; Media Researcher: Rebekah Hubstenberger; Production Specialist: Tori Abraham

Image Credits
Alamy: Roger De Marfà, 20, PA Images/Jane Barlow, 15; Capstone: Jon Hughes, 1, 4, 8, 12, 13, 16, 17, 19, 21, 23, 25; Getty Images: Corey Ford/Stocktrek Images, 18, 24, Dan Kitwood, 28, iStock/wwing, 26, Mark Stevenson/Stocktrek Images, 22; Science Source: Francois Gohier, 27; Shutterstock: Catmando, 5, 11, Daniel Eskridge, 10, 14, Herschel Hoffmeyer, 7, KRagona, 6, Kues (background), cover and throughout, Warpaint, cover

Printed and bound in China. 006276

Table of Contents

Words in **bold** are in the glossary.

Long-Necked Giant

Imagine traveling back to the time of the dinosaurs. Feel the ground shake! A Diplodocus walks by. This giant dinosaur is as long as three school buses. Look out for its long neck. Its tail is even longer!

Diplodocus was part of a group of huge dinosaurs named Sauropods. Diplodocus lived around 150 million years ago. This time was near the end of the **Jurassic** Period.

Where in the World

Diplodocus lived in what is now the western United States. Dinosaur hunters have found Diplodocus **fossils** in Colorado, Utah, Wyoming, and Montana. Fossils of many dinosaurs have been discovered in this area.

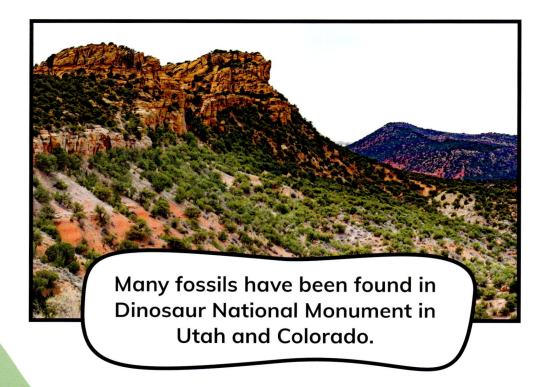

Many fossils have been found in Dinosaur National Monument in Utah and Colorado.

This area is now grassland and mountains. But in the Jurassic Period, North America was very different.

The area where Diplodocus lived was **wetland**. Rivers crossed the land. The **climate** was different too. Bushes and trees grew in warm, wet forests.

Diplodocus shared the forests with other large, plant-eating dinosaurs. One of them was Apatosaurus. Fierce meat-eaters such as Allosaurus also prowled around.

Diplodocus Bodies

Diplodocus was one of the longest animals that ever lived. The biggest Diplodocus was more than 100 feet (30 meters) from its head to the tip of its tail.

Diplodocus's skin color is not known. Its skin could have been striped.

Diplodocus weighed between 11 and 17 tons. That is about the same as three African elephants. But Diplodocus weighed less than other large dinosaurs. It had a lighter **skeleton** because bones in its back were hollow.

Diplodocus stood on four sturdy legs. The front legs were shorter than the back ones. Its wide feet had five toes.

Did You Know?

Some scientists think that Diplodocus had bony spikes along its back.

Its **spine** had more than 100 bones. Strong cords held the spine together. The cords are called **ligaments**. They controlled the dinosaur's long neck and tail.

Diplodocus moved with its huge tail stretched out behind it. The tail could be up to 45 feet (14 m) long. It was covered in sharp scales or spikes.

Diplodocus's head was very small. Its neck could only hold up a small head. Its brain was even smaller. The brain weighed about 4 ounces (113 grams). That's a bit less than a baseball.

A museum worker cleans a Diplodocus skull.

What Diplodocus Ate

   Diplodocus ate plants. It fed on ferns and bushes close to the ground. It could also stretch its long neck to eat leaves from tall trees. Other dinosaurs could not reach that high.

Diplodocus could stand on its back
legs. This helped it stretch even higher.
Its tail rested on the ground for balance.

Diplodocus had straight teeth, like a comb. They were all at the front of its mouth. The teeth were not very strong. They broke often. New teeth would grow to take their place.

Did You Know?

Diplodocus grew new teeth about once a month.

Diplodocus had no back teeth. It could not chew its food. It swallowed its food whole.

Life of Diplodocus

A baby Diplodocus hatched from an egg. This egg was as big as a grapefruit. Small groups of Diplodocus laid their eggs together.

A Diplodocus egg

A young Diplodocus grew up deep in the forest. This protected it from attack by other dinosaurs.

Diplodocus grew quickly. After four years, it was as long as a small truck. A Diplodocus could take 25 years to reach full size.

Predators threatened young Diplodocus. Ceratosaurus and Allosaurus were meat-eaters. They might eat eggs. But they could only hunt small dinosaurs. A fully grown Diplodocus was too big to attack.

Did You Know?

Diplodocus might have used its huge tail as a whip. It could fight off other dinosaurs.

Diplodocus may have lived in small groups. They protected each other from predators. The herd worked together to find food. A hungry Diplodocus needed plenty to eat!

Diplodocus was slower than many dinosaurs. It moved between 5 and 10 miles (8 and 15 kilometers) per hour. Moving that big body took lots of energy. Diplodocus stayed still when it could. It grabbed all the food within reach. Then it moved on.

Discovering Diplodocus

Scientists learn about dinosaurs from fossils. Bones, footprints, and even poop can become fossils. Scientists have found nearly complete skeletons of Diplodocus. This helps them learn about this dinosaur.

Fossil poop is called coprolite.

The first Diplodocus fossil was found near Cañon City, Colorado, in 1877. Scientist O. C. Marsh named the new discovery Diplodocus. The name means "double beamed." It comes from the shape of the dinosaur's tail bones.

A scientist digs up a Diplodocus fossil in Wyoming.

In 1898, William Harlow Reed found a Diplodocus skeleton in Wyoming. His team dug it up. It was rebuilt in Pittsburgh, Pennsylvania. People named it Dippy.

Copies of the skeleton were sent to museums around the world. Dippy is one of the most famous dinosaurs ever found.

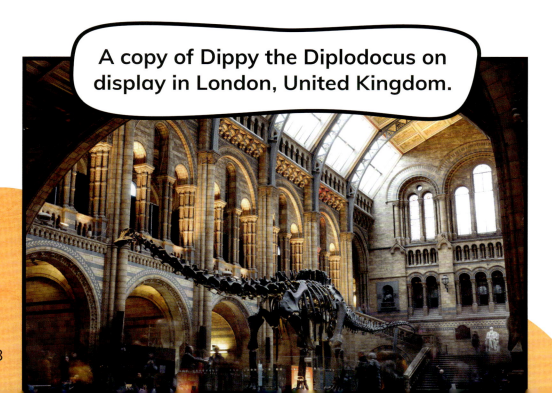

A copy of Dippy the Diplodocus on display in London, United Kingdom.

Fast Facts

Name: Diplodocus (meaning "double beamed")

Lived: Late Jurassic Period
(156 to 142 million years ago)

Range: Western United States (Utah, Colorado, Wyoming, Montana)

Habitat: Warm, wet forests

Food: Leaves and plant material

Threats: Allosaurus, Ceratosaurus

Discovered: Cañon City, Colorado, 1877

Glossary

climate (KLAI-mut)—the usual weather conditions in a region

fossil (FAH-suhl)—the remains or traces of a living thing from many years ago

Jurassic (juh-RA-sic)—the period of Earth's history when many dinosaurs were alive, beginning around 201 million years ago and ending 145 million years ago

ligament (LI-guh-munt)—a band of tough, flexible material connecting bones together

predator (PRED-uh-tur)—an animal that hunts other animals for food

skeleton (SKEL-uh-tun)—the structure of bones that supports the body of an animal

spine (SPYN)—a series of small bones connected together down an animal's back

wetland (WET-land)—a swampy or marshy area of land

Read More

Clausen-Grace, Nicki. *Diplodocus*. Mankato, MN: Black Rabbit Books, 2024.

Gregory, Josh. *Discover the Diplodocus*. Ann Arbor, MI: Cherry Lake Publishing, 2023.

National Geographic. *Dinosaur Atlas: When They Roamed, How They Lived, and Where We Find Their Fossils*. Washington, DC: National Geographic, 2022.

Internet Sites

American Museum of Natural History: Dinosaurs
amnh.org/dinosaurs

Britannica Kids: Diplodocus
kids.britannica.com/kids/article/Diplodocus/390034

Natural History Museum: Diplodocus
nhm.ac.uk/discover/dino-directory/diplodocus.html

Index

About the Author

Nick Hunter has written more than 100 books for young people, including several on dinosaurs and prehistoric life. He is fascinated by the way that scientists learn about dinosaurs by studying fossils. New discoveries are being made all the time. Nick lives in Oxford, United Kingdom, with his wife and two sons.